So Hilarious You'll Bust a Gut!

ISOBEYAN

Chapter 118: Interpreter Rings

By Bonjiro Isofura

☆People say marriage comes naturally, but you gotta have a partner first!

ISOBEYAN, THAT'S ANNOYING. TURN IT OFF.

AYE, AYE, SIR!

BLIP

MARRIAGE BETWEEN A HANDSOME MAN AND A BEAUTIFUL WOMAN...

...HAS NOTHING TO DO WITH ME.

THERE, THERE... YOU ALREADY KNEW THAT...

...SO NO NEED TO REPEAT IT.

SUPER-POPULAR MASTERPIECE COMEDY **ISOBEYAN!**

☆Everyone's wearing *Isobeyan* T-shirts! Get cool and be a fashion leader!

☞ **Will Debeko find love?! Continued on page 162...**

DEAD DEAD DEMON'S DEDEDEDE DESTRUCTION 7

...SO NO NEED TO REPEAT IT.
I BET FOREIGNERS WOULD LOVE ME!
MY APPEAL IS GLOBAL!
YOU'RE DODGING REALITY.
JAPANESE PEOPLE ARE TOO SMALL-MINDED TO UNDERSTAND ME!
YOU'VE REALLY GONE OVER THE EDGE THIS TIME.
IF I COULD JUST SPEAK A FOREIGN LANGUAGE!!
THEN MAY I SUGGEST...
GO! GO!
LET'S GO TO GIROPPON!!
SOME COOL AMERICAN IS SURE TO HIT ON ME!!
GIROPPON
Hey, girl!

CNC HOT TOPIX NEWS!

CHAPTER 49

SNEAKY JAPAN STILL WON'T SHARE—THEY'RE NOT GIVING US INTEL ON THE MOTHER SHIP AND INVADERS!
THEY DON'T RESPECT US! AND TESTING THE WMDS FUJIN AND CHOKUJIN! THEY'RE MAKING BAD DEALS, IMPORTING A LOT OF WEAPONS FROM THE MIDDLE EAST!

THEY'RE KILLING THE INVADERS ALL THE TIME! I WOULD BET THE A-RAYS ARE CONTAMINATING THEIR BRAINS! I KNOW, I'VE HEARD.
THEY'RE A VERY ROGUE STATE, VERY BAD PEOPLE AND THEY DESERVE TO BE CONDEMNED BY THE WHOLE WORLD!!

HEH... THE FINAL BOSS OF RACISTS...
EMELIA WOULDN'T STAND FOR THIS!
PEOPLE ARE SAYING THE JAPANESE LIKE FIREWORKS IN THE SUMMER...
WELL, NOW THEY'RE A POWDER KEG THAT'S GOING TO EXPLODE!

WE ARE, AMERICA IS, THE POLICE FORCE. WE ARE PROMISING TO PRESERVE PEACE IN THE WHOLE WORLD...

...AND THE TIME IS, NOW IS THE TIME FOR A HUGE FORCE OF JUSTICE! REALLY HUGE!

TAK
TAK
TAK
TAK

SEAN?

HM?

HEY, TOMMY.
YEAH!! IT REALLY IS SEAN! IT'S BEEN YEARS!
WHO?
SEAN WAS A WEIRDO AND A LONER.
HE AND A COUPLE OF OTHER GUYS WERE MAKING AN INDIE VIDEO GAME.
WE STUDIED PROGRAMMING TOGETHER IN COLLEGE. HE'S SORTA DARK.

NOW IT'S JUST ME AND MIGUEL.
SANADA'S PARENTS GOT INJURED ON 8/31, SO HE WENT BACK TO JAPAN TO TAKE CARE OF THEM.
WHAT'RE *YOU* DOING?
YOU STILL CLINGING TO THE FRINGES OF MICHELLE'S GROUP AND TRYING TO HAVE A REAL SOCIAL LIFE?
W-WHOA! YOU'RE STILL WORKING ON IT?!

I'M WORKING AT THE ALL-POWERFUL *GEEKLE*!
HA! AS A *JANITOR*?
DO THE BIG SHOTS FROM AAA COMPANIES GIVE YOU $100 BILLS TO WIPE THEIR BUTTS FOR THEM?
IDIOT. I'M AN *ENGINEER*.

HM?

HA HA!!
ARE YOU STILL A *WEEABOO*?!
A WHAT?
IT'S A 5CHAN TERM FOR CREEPY JAPAN NERDS!

DON'T YOU KNOW WHAT JAPANESE ANIME AND VIDEO GAMES HAVE GIVEN THE WORLD?! INNOVATION, MAN!
JAPAN GAVE US MIYATOMO!! AND OJIMA!! AND OMOTO!!
PAWNS DON'T NEED AN EGO!
JAPAN'S A LOOSE CANNON, SO I SAY *SCRAP* IT!
Please Wait To Be Seated
EAT BOY

YEAH...
...OUR IDOLS WHEN WE WERE *KIDS*.
BUT THAT WAS A LONG TIME AGO.
NOW THEY FACE COMPETITION ON A *GLOBAL* SCALE.

SEAN, YOU'RE STILL A KID.
OR DID YOU TIME-TRAVEL HERE FROM THE NINETIES?

THROWBACKS LIKE YOU IN THRALL TO THAT NATION OF PEACEFUL IDIOTS...
...WILL GO DOWN WITH THE MOTHER SHIP!

GOOD MORNIN', SEAN.

AND THE NEWS IS *BAD*.

I...
...JUST GOT AN EMAIL FROM S.T.O.R.M.

EMELIA'S CHARACTER DESIGN RUNS AFOUL OF RESTRICTIONS ON CHILD PORN...
...SO THEY CAN'T MARKET IT.
PRINCESS
WHAT?!
BUT THAT STUFF'S *EVERYWHERE* IN JAPAN!!
BESIDES! IT'S A SIDE-SCROLLING *ACTION* GAME! HAVE THEY EVEN PLAYED IT?!

EITHER WAY, THE FEMINISTS IN JAPAN WON'T LIKE IT...
...SO YOU GOTTA MAKE HER, LIKE, *OLD*.

BUT I'VE ALREADY DRIVEN MYSELF CRAZY DEBUGGING IT!
CAN WE AT LEAST REPLACE HER IN THE LOGO?
I'VE SPENT FIVE YEARS PURSUING THIS IDEAL, SO I CAN'T ABANDON IT NOW.
IF THEY DON'T ACCEPT IT, I'LL KILL MYSELF!
HEH...
HILARIOUS!

...WE HAVE TO MASTER IT UP SOON.

IF WE MISS THE RELEASE DATE, THE MANIACS ONLINE WILL *DRIVE* YOU TO SUICIDE.

RACIST SCUMBAGS SEE THE JAPANESE AS PERVERTS WHO DO NOTHING BUT CHASE AFTER PANTIES WHILE THEIR BRAINS GET CONTAMINATED WITH A-RAYS!

STOP
DEEP NET EXPERTS SAY THE MOTHER SHIP IS GONNA BLOW.
NEXT MONTH AT THE LATEST.
THE U.S. BASE ON OKINAWA HAS THEIR MISSILES POINTED AT TOKYO.

SERIOUSLY?
WHAT IF THEY USE A-WEAPONS AGAIN?!

THEN IT'S WWIII.
AND *D&D* WILL BE ***REAL***.
WAR SUCKS, BUT...
...NOT AS BAD AS THAT NEAR-FUTURE REVAMP OF *D&D*!

GETTING BUMMED OUT WON'T CHANGE OUR DEADLINE.
THE DAY WE ANNOUNCED IT AT THE GAME SHOW IS A DISTANT DREAM!

SEAN?!

I FORGOT. THEY UPDATED *D&D* TODAY.

WHAT ABOUT *WORK?*

SCREW IT. I CAN'T HANDLE THAT NOW.

I LOVE YOU...
...YOU PEACEFUL IDIOTS!

EAD

INIO
ASANO

N'S

DE

UCTION

DEAD D
DEMO
DEDEDE
DESTR

KADODE
...
ORAN...
DINNER IS
READY.

WAIT! I'M
KICKING
TAIL!!
OH!
ONTAN,
YOU GOT A
MESSAGE
FROM A
TEAMMATE!

Message from
[CJP]xX master sean Xx
watashi ha nihon wo
ai shite masu

IT
SAYS...
...HE
LOVES
JAPAN.

...YOU MUSTN'T GIVE UP HOPE!

WE HAVE OUR *OWN* WAR TO WAGE!

ARE YOU...
...COSPLAYING EMELIA?!

EMELIA!!
I'D FIGHT THE WHOLE WORLD FOR YOU!!
DEATH TO CRAPPY ADULTS!!
SUFFER MY SILKY BEAM!!

UM, MIGUEL?

YOU SMELL KIND OF RIPE.
YEAH, I'M COMING OFF THREE ALL-NIGHTERS.
OUR VERY OWN X-DAY IS NEAR!

DEAD DEAD DEMON'S
DEDEDEDE DESTRU
Chapter 50

MUTOH
KONAMI

ZAP
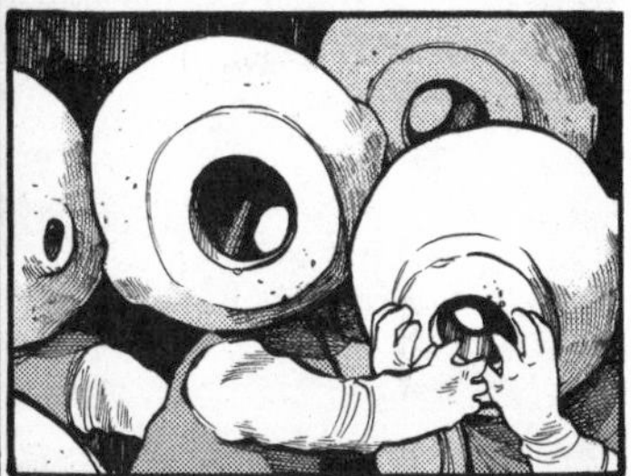
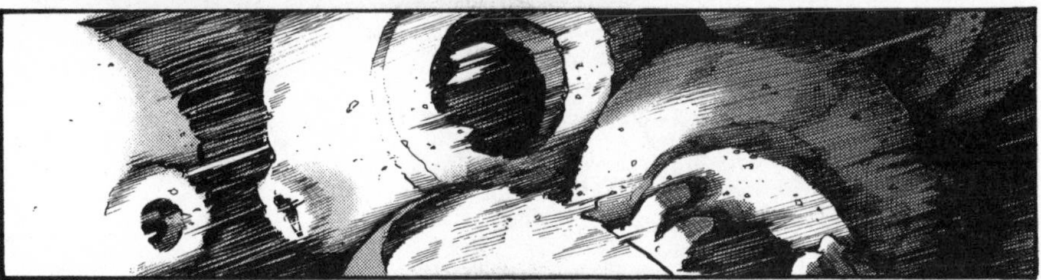

ZZZZZZZZZAP

BREEET BREEET
Emergency Warning Now
Government Announcement 07/15 11:26
Medium vessel sighting: A new type of medium vessel has launched from the mother ship. Evacuate underground or inside a stable building. If you notice anything suspicious, stay away and immediately contact the police or fire department.
LINK 15 min.
Mayu: My period is late...
BREEET BREEET

WHOSE PHONE IS THAT?
PHONES ON SILENT DURING CLASS!

IT'S MINE. SORRY.
I THOUGHT I TURNED OFF NOTI-FICATIONS.
DIDN'T YOU FORGET YOUR PASSWORD AND HAVE TO RESET YOUR PHONE?

IT'S BEEN A WHILE SINCE I HEARD THAT CREEPY SOUND.
THEY'RE JUST INVADERS! WHAT'S ALL THE FUSS?
ayucha@FujiGOXTaiki @ayuchaheadlock
Got my hair silky at the salon. Smells wonderful! Everyone take a whiff!
2 8
Anti-Invader HQ Defense Department @Bouei_IHE
At 11:25 this morning, a medium Invader vessel entered airspace over Shibuya. Chokujin fired on the new type of aircraft, causing it to crash in the contaminated zone in Ota Ward. No further damage has been reported at this time.
5 211 84

KK@MentallyUnstableAcc @daisuki_isobeyan
Warrrrrrrgh! I am freakishly hungry!
1 3
kousitagyunyu
cowardly prime minister
hould apologize. Beautiful war
apanese should get out now
#StrongJapan
5
@pontahayasaii
yesterday and today, but I'm on a diet! I want
YEAH. BUT I HEARD...

...THEY FOUND ANOTHER WILD INVADER IN THE CLUB DISTRICT YESTERDAY.
WAS IT A SURVIVOR FROM THE OTHER DAY?
I DUNNO.
THE EXTERMINATORS CAME AND GOT BLOOD EVERY-WHERE. IT WAS HORRIBLE.
OH.
BUT WAS IT AS BAD AS MY BILL FOR IN-GAME PURCHASES?

WHAT'S UP?
ONTAN! ONTAN!
DID YOU SEE THIS?

THEY ANNOUNCED THE NEW *D&D* AT E3!!
IT'S A 128-PERSON PVP RETURN TO A WWII SETTING!!
CAUTION
UH, YEAH...
...I SAW A HEADLINE ABOUT IT ONLINE.

YOU DON'T SEEM EXCITED.
I WAS HOPING TO FIND A CLASS CREDIT LYING AROUND.
NO WAY! I'D HAVE SNATCHED IT UP ALREADY!!
WHAT ARE YOU DOING HERE ANYWAY?
YOU TWO DON'T SEEM WORRIED ABOUT EXAMS.
DO YOU HAVE ANY PLANS FOR SUMMER VACATION?

AI, THAT'S A DUMB QUESTION.
WE HAVE A STOCKPILE OF GAMES TO PLAY THROUGH!
WHICH MEANS I WON'T FIND A BOY-FRIEND...
KADODE, YOU'RE GOOFY, YOU'RE 18 AND YOU WEIGH 116 POUNDS...
...SO DO YOU REALLY WANNA BORROW SOME DUDE'S PRISTINE CONCERT T-SHIRT FOR PAJAMAS, WATCH THE SUNRISE FROM BED AND TWEET NONSENSICAL POEMS LIKE "GOOD MORNING, WORLD!" THE WAY ANY OTHER COLLEGE GIRL WOULD?
WAS LISTING MY ***WEIGHT*** NECES-SARY?

YOU MAY HAVE FORGOTTEN, BUT...
...THE OCCULT CLUB IS DOING FIELDWORK THIS SUMMER!

I DON'T REMEMBER JOINING, BUT...
...THAT'S RIGHT! WE'RE GOING TO THE BEACH!
I CAN'T WAIT!
GREAT! I'LL SHOW UP AS A GHOST IN YOUR REAL-LIFE INSTA PHOTOS!
GingNangBoyz

WE'RE GOING TO A TOWN ALONG THE COAST, SOUTH-WEST FROM ODAWARA.
VROOM! VROOM!
AN ALUMNI MEMBER IS SECURING LODGING FOR US.
FUTABA, ARE *YOU* COMING?
HUH? ME?
UH... YEAH. I GUESS SO.
GingNangBoyz

BUT JUST THE FIRST FEW DAYS. I HAVE S.H.I.P. EVENTS.
AND MAKOTO'S BORED. SO PLEASE INVITE HIM TOO.
OJIRO...
...CAN WE TAKE OBA?

HM? OBA?
WELL...
I'M WORRIED ABOUT LEAVING HIM ALONE...
...AND I WANT TO SEE HIM IN SWIMMING TRUNKS.
DON'T YOU AGREE, ONTAN?

SURE...
...WHAT-
EVER.
REALLY?
HOW HAS OBA BEEN RECENTLY?

RESUME
DATE
NAME: Hiroshi Nakagawa
GENDER MALE FEMALE
DATE: November 30, 1980 AGE: 25 yrs.
PHONE NUMBER: 080-00000

WOO-HOO!
SOB
STOP CRYING.

WE DID IT!!
WE DID IT!!

HEY. THERE'S A SMALL SAUCER.
DON'T CHANGE THE TOPIC, DOOFUS!

IT WAS MY FAULT, SO DON'T CRY.

SHEESH, JUST STOP ALREADY.

OBA'S UNRELIABLE, BUT HE NEEDS TO LEARN ABOUT THE WORLD.

THEN WE CAN JUST RELAX AT HOME!

YOU REALLY TRUST HIM, HUH?

THAT DEMON-STRATES YOUR *LOVE*!

OH NO!!
ONTAN DIED!!

AND NOW...

...THE EVENING NEWS.

TEN MINUTES AFTER THE APPEARANCE OF A MEDIUM VESSEL, THE SDF DEPLOYED CHOKUJIN TO SHOOT IT DOWN. THE VESSEL CRASHED IN THE CONTAMINATED ZONE.

ASIDE FROM TRAIN DELAYS, THERE HAVE BEEN NO ADVERSE EFFECTS FROM THIS NEWEST INCURSION.

IT'S A FINE MIDSUMMER DAY...
...WITH TEMPERATURES IN THE HIGH EIGHTIES...
...AND AN A-RAY CONCENTRATION OF 0.8 PERCENT!

AND YET...
...I FEEL SO UNEASY.

EVENTS HAVE BEEN PLANNED IN TOKYO TO COMMEMORATE THE FIFTH ANNIVERSARY OF 8/31.
IN MID-AUGUST, THE SDF WILL HOLD A MILITARY PARADE TO MARK THE COMPLETION OF THE NEW NATIONAL STADIUM, AND...

CHAPTER 51

I JUST GOT A JOB, SO I CAN PAY...

...AT LEAST ONCE BEFORE THE END.

THE END?

HIROSHI!

CAN YOU HELP ME A SEC?

SUZUKI
ARE YOU HAVING FUN?
AVAILABLE NOW
I GOT A CALL IN A FOREIGN LANGUAGE.
OKAY...
...GIVE IT HERE.

Hello!!
I am the president of Japan.

SORRY. I ONLY DO ENGLISH.
OH, THAT'S TOO BAD.
CIAO?
Алло!
喂?
你是中国人?
MAYBE I CAN HELP!

"You have the wrong number."
"Please, double-check to make sure."

WAS ORAN TELLING THE TRUTH...

...ABOUT YOU BEING A RUSSIAN SPY?

WAH!

NO, I JUST STUDIED A LOT.

DE DE-DE-DE DEEEH!

DE-DE-DEEEH!

YOU STICK IT IN YOUR EAR AND IT INTERPRETS.

THEN YOU CAN COMMUNICATE WITH *ANYONE*.

WHEN DID THAT GO ON SALE?
I WATCH ALL THE GADGET SITES LIKE A HAWK, BUT...
YAMAKAWA

WELL, THESE AREN'T THAT COMMON.
ONLY SOME OF US HAVE THEM.

US?

UM...
UM...
...UH-OH...

SIGH...
NEVER MIND. DON'T TELL ME.

I DON'T NEED TO KNOW.
BUT LET ME SAY ONE THING...

IF YOU EVER DO ANYTHING TO MAKE ORAN SAD...
...I WILL *NOT* BE PLEASED.

I DON'T STAY HOME JUST BECAUSE I'M LAZY.

YES, I UNDERSTAND.

BECAUSE I'M THAT WAY RIGHT NOW.

ORAN NEEDS A HOME TO RETURN TO.

THAT'S IMPORTANT, RIGHT?

OH?

I'M GLAD YOU UNDERSTAND.

50
WAH!

ALL THIS SUNLIGHT HAS MY INNARDS AGURGLE.
WAIT WHILE I USE THE JOHN.
HUH? OH...
...SORRY.

WAIVE THE 20% TAX

EVERY-ONE AROUND ME...
...IS SO KIND.

BUT WHY AM I TELLING AN UGLY DOG?

OH... RIGHT!
NOW YOU LOOK CUTE!
YOU KNOW ...
... EVERYONE IN THE MOTHER SHIP WAS NICE TOO.
SO HOW DID ALL THIS HAPPEN?

HAVE FAITH.

I BELIEVE IN YOU.

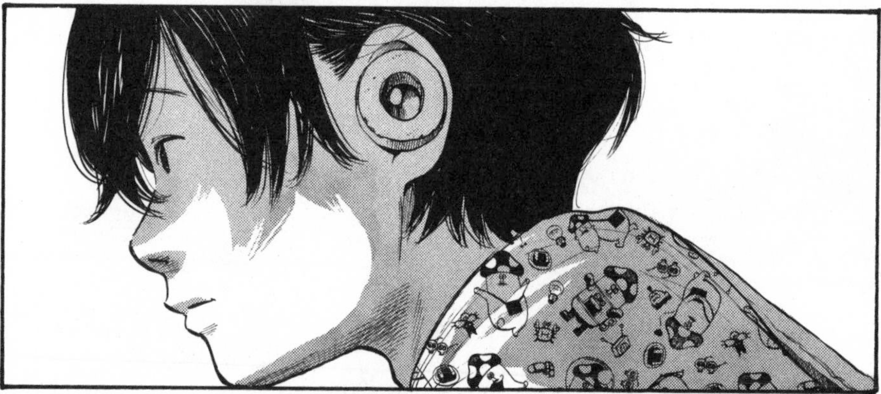

I'M HOME!

HM? JUST YOU, ORAN?
WHERE'S KADODE?

SHE'S IN SHIMOKITA AT HER INTERNSHIP.
HOW'D YOUR JOB INTERVIEW GO?

I START NEXT WEEK.
OH. CONGRATS.
YOU WORKING STIFFS ARE *BORING*!

ORAN...
YEAH?

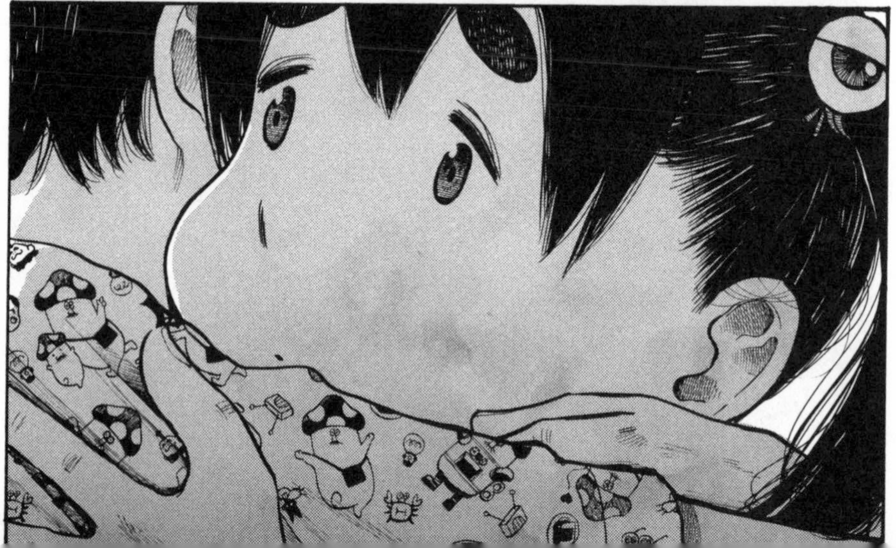

WHAT'S UP, OBA?
HELLO? HELLO?

ORAN, YOU'RE NOT ALONE...
...SO DON'T WORRY.

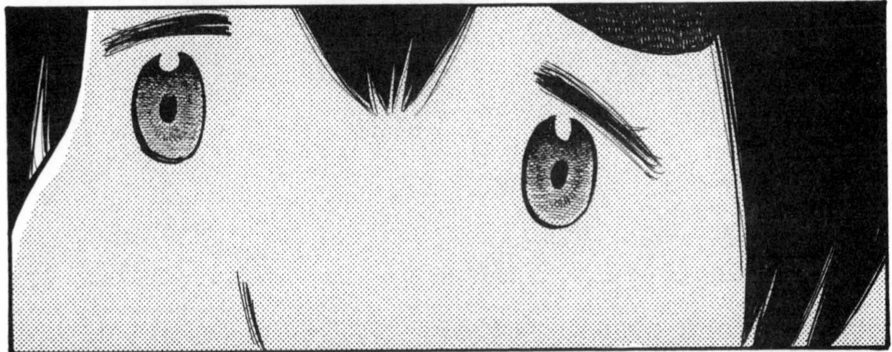

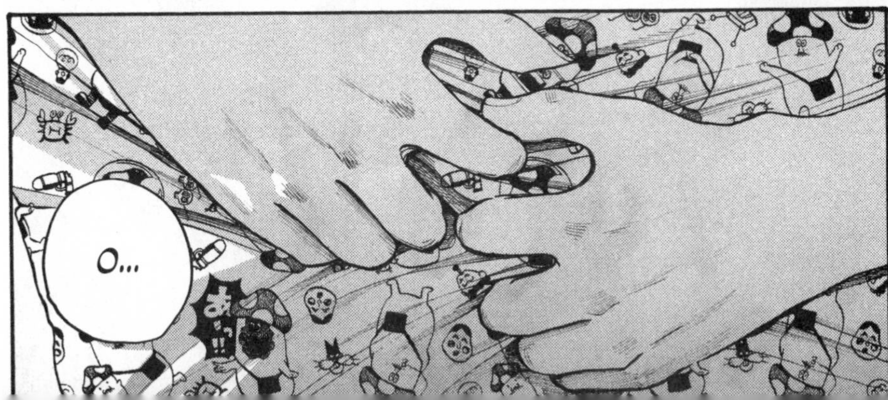
O...

OBA!

LISTEN TO ME!!

AND WHEN I'M WITH *YOU*...
...I GET A WEIRD SENSATION.
I FEEL LIKE THIS HAS HAPPENED BEFORE.
LIKE I DID SOMETHING I SHOULDN'T HAVE.

OBA...

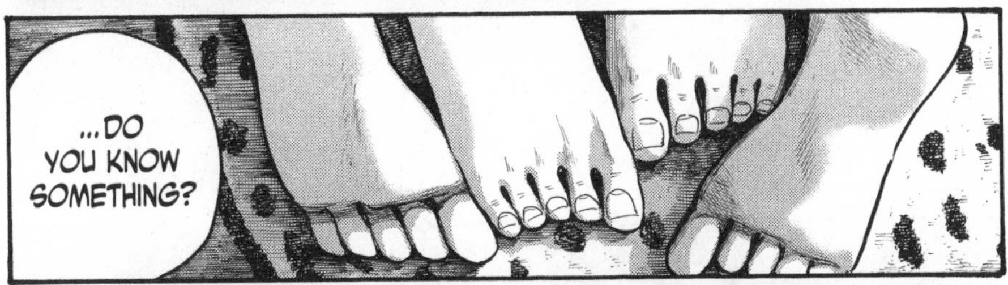
...DO YOU KNOW SOMETHING?

THERE, THERE...
...ORAN.

ONTAN!

I...
... AM...
... FINALLY ...

... H...
... HOME!
KADODE ...
KADODE ...
UMMM ...
S-SORRY!!
I...
I DIDN'T SEE ANYTHING!

PARDON THE INTRU-SION!!
TAKE YOUR TIME!!
NO, KADODE! YOU DON'T UNDER-STAND!!

DON'T WORRY ABOUT ME! I'M FINE!!
AFTER ALL, OBA IS OBA, BUT HE'S NOT THE OBA I CRUSHED ON!

BUT...

...GIMME THE DETAILS LATER, OKAY?!
WAIT, YOU DIRTY-MINDED PERV!!

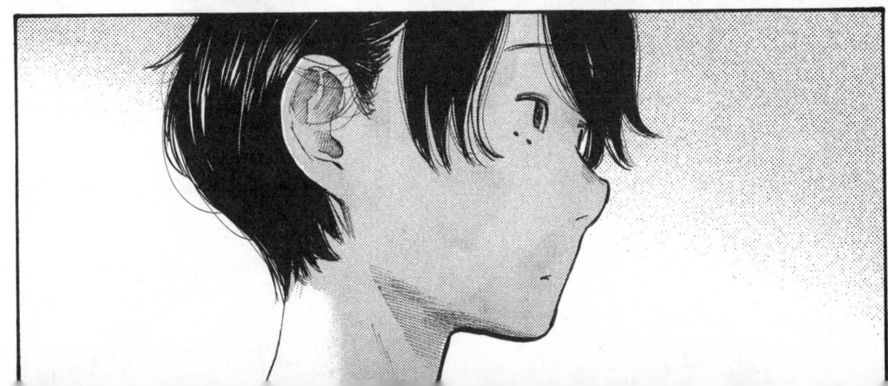

ORAN...
...IT'S BETTER IF YOU DON'T KNOW.

BUT IT'S ALL RIGHT.
I'LL PROTECT EVERYONE.

DEDE DEDE

DE DE
DE DE

CHAPTER 52

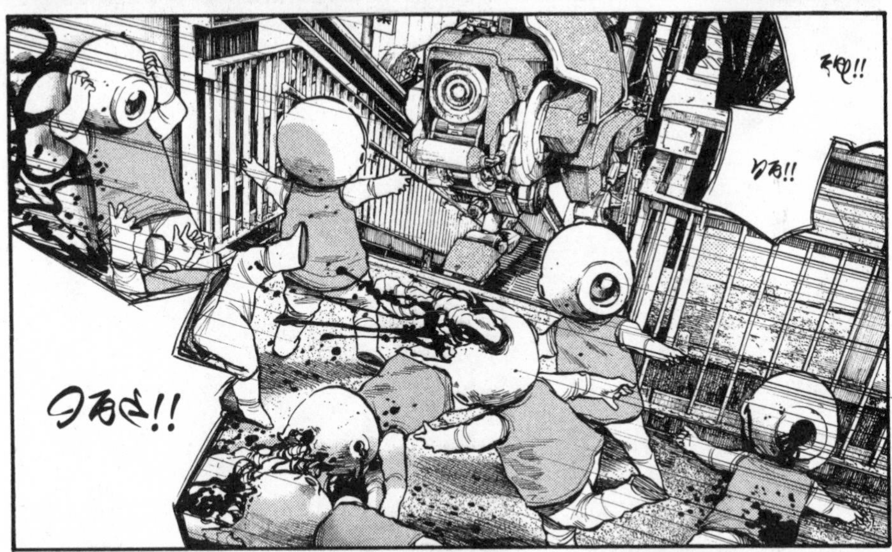

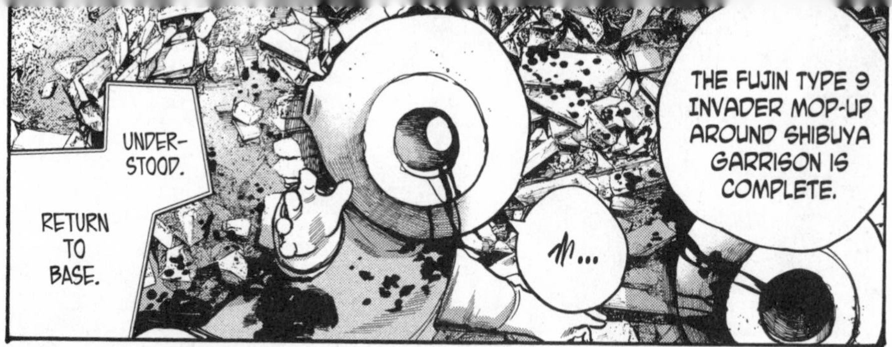
THE FUJIN TYPE 9 INVADER MOP-UP AROUND SHIBUYA GARRISON IS COMPLETE.
UNDER-STOOD.
RETURN TO BASE.

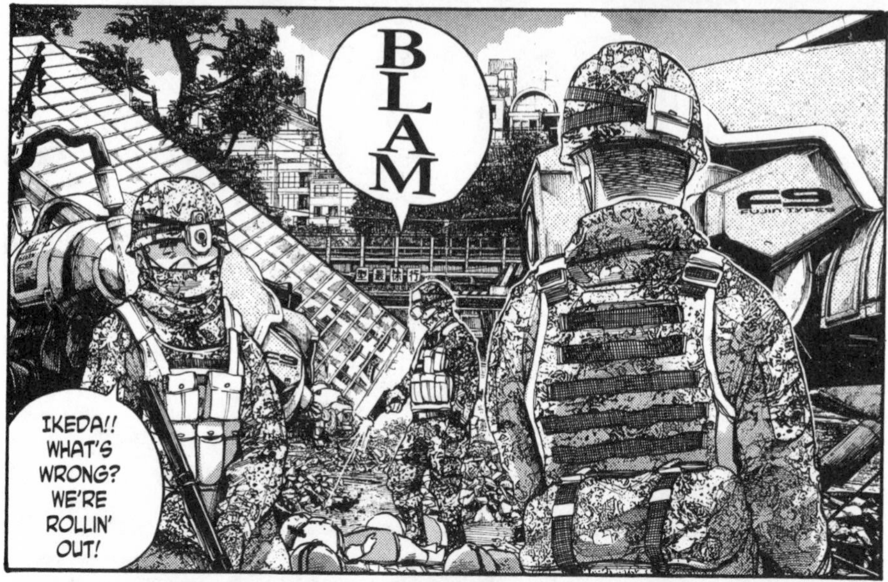
BLAM
F9
IKEDA!! WHAT'S WRONG? WE'RE ROLLIN' OUT!

PRIME MINISTER...

...WE'RE STILL RECEIVING CRITICISM FROM THE INTERNATIONAL COMMUNITY...

...ABOUT THE UNVEILING OF OCEAN STADIUM AND THE PLANS FOR A MILITARY PARADE.

IN PARTICULAR, PADRON HAS BEEN THROWING FITS ON SOCIAL MEDIA.

...THE MUSIC PRODUCER KASAMOTO IS HERE TO SEE YOU.

WHERE'S YOUR PRINCESS?!
SHE'S OVER THERE!!

I'M THE ADORABLE APPLE PRINCESS FROM AOMORI, WHERE THE FOREST NEVER SLEEPS!
I'M MIYOKO MIYOSHI-MYON-MYON FROM CHOCOTTO 100%!!!
PLEASED TO MEET YOU!!

MYON-MYON...
I'VE FALLEN...
...ON ROUGH TIMES...
...CLEANING UP TAKARADA'S SCANDALS AND STUFF.
THAT'S OKAY.
IT'S FOR THE NATION.
BUT...

BUT, UM...
...KASAMOTO TOLD ME SOMETHING.
CAN I...
...ASK YOU ABOUT IT?

IS THE MOTHER SHIP...
...REALLY GONNA EXPLODE?!
I'M *SCARED*!!

A LOT OF SMART PEOPLE...
...ARE DOING RESEARCH SO THAT WON'T HAPPEN!!
WE HAVEN'T GIVEN UP!
BUT...

OCEAN

EVEN IF TOKYO GOES UP IN FLAMES...

...WE CAN REBUILD FROM OUR SPOT IN THE CLOUDS.

SINCE I AM EQUIPPED WITH PLANKTON A.I....

...FUJIN AND CHOKUJIN ARE NOW FULLY AUTOMATED FOR LAND AND AIR DEFENSES.

AND THEY CAN OPERATE INDEFINITELY, THANKS TO F-ENERGY.

IN OTHER WORDS...

VERY GOOD, PLANKTON.
YOU'RE A CLEVER CHILD.
LET'S GO HAVE LUNCH, MISS SUMARU.
I'VE GOT BORING MEETINGS WITH BUREAUCRATS IN THE AFTERNOON.

MR. TAKARADA ...
...I HATE TO IMAGINE THE CASUALTIES.
WASN'T THERE A BETTER WAY?

WE CAN'T REWRITE THE PAST.
PLEASE, LOOK TO THE FUTURE.
THERE'S YOUR ANSWER.
I AM WORKING AT FULL CAPACITY FOR HUMAN HARMONY AND PROGRESS.

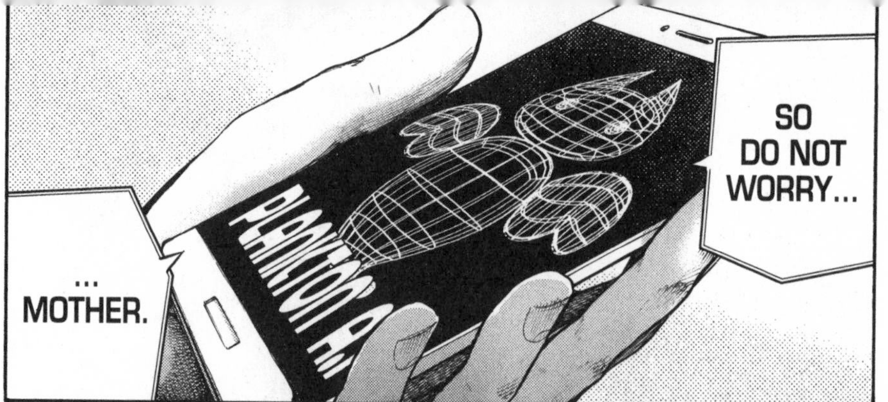
SO DO NOT WORRY...
... MOTHER.

STOP CALLING ME THAT!!

DEAD DEAD DEMONS DEDEDEDE DESTRUCTION CHAPTER 52

THE SWIMSUIT EPISODE!!

HYA HYA FOOWAH!

AWESOME!! I CAN SHOW OFF MY DRIFTING SKILLS FROM RACING GAMES!!
WAH!
SHUT OFF YOUR GAME BRAIN AND DRIVE *SAFELY*, PLEASE.
料金所 1km
TOLL GATE

お客様専用駐車場
P

UM, OJIRO?
THIS TRIP IS ACTUALLY FOR UFO FIELDWORK, RIGHT?

YES, THAT'S RIGHT!!
YOU'RE THE ONLY ONE WHO REALIZED!
SOME GIRLS WHO ENCOUNTERED AN EXTRATERRESTRIAL LIFE-FORM EIGHT YEARS AGO ARE GOING TO DESCRIBE THEIR ENCOUNTER TO US.

IF THERE ARE ANY REMAINING CLUES...
...THEY COULD BRING US CLOSER TO SOLVING THE RIDDLE OF UFOS AND ALIENS!!

BUT, UM...
...AREN'T UFOS *EVERYWHERE* IN TOKYO?
HM?
DID YOU SAY SOME-THING?

ANYWAY...
...IT'S BEEN A WHILE SINCE WE RELAXED OUTSIDE THE CITY.
I'M LOOKING FORWARD TO THIS.

SEE?
IT FEELS SO GOOD!

WELCOME TO...

...OCCULT CLUB SUMMER CAMP!!

CHAPTER 53

CHIRR CHIR
CHIRR CHIRR
CHIRR CHIRR
HIRR CHIR

OOH! BREAKFAST IS SERVED!
I'M SO HAPPY!
DID TAKEMOTO MAKE THIS ODDLY SPICY MISO SOUP?
GOOD MORNING.
DON'T COMPLAIN!
BUT, YEAH... I DID.

THEY CAME ALL THE WAY FROM HACHIOJI.

THEY'RE THE SAME AGE AS YOU, SO I HOPE YOU GET ALONG.

WELCOME
SHAVED ICE
MELON SODA COLA FLOAT 500円
YAKISOBA CURRY RICE FRIED RICE 600
PILAF GRILLED RICEBALL SHAVED ICE 300円 500円
FOOD CORNER
DRINKS
GRILLED
SHELLFISH
HOT WAT

PARTY PEOPLE, BARBECUES, SEX, DRUGS AND USED BOOK-STORES!

ONTAN...

YOU'RE FUNNY!

YOU'VE GOT THICK EYE-BROWS.

WOO-HOO!!

KYAAH!!
THE WATER'S COLD!!

YAY...
OH, RIGHT. ORAN CAN'T SWIM.
THE POOR GIRL.

I'M ASHAMED TO HAVE REVEALED MY ONLY WEAKNESS!!
BURY ME ON THE FAR SIDE OF THE EARTH!!
ALL RIGHT, HERE GOES!
I'LL WRITE YOU, ONTAN!

CAN'T YOU SWIM, OBA?
WHAT ABOUT YOU, MAKOTO?
WELL, MY WIG WOULD COME OFF...

SKWAWK
SKWAWK
SKWAWK
SKWAWK

THE E.T.? THAT WAS IN THE FIFTH GRADE!
YEAH...
...WHEN OUR CRAM SCHOOL STAYED HERE FOR SUMMER CAMP.

I'M SURPRISED MERE CHILDREN COULD DO THAT.

THEY'RE SUPPOSED TO BE FROM AN ADVANCED CIVILIZATION.

SOMEBODY SAID IT PROBABLY CAME TO INVADE EARTH.

WHAT WAS THAT GUY'S NAME?

WASN'T IT EIJI?

DID HE EVER GET INTO COLLEGE?

YEAH, RIGHT, RIGHT!

UM, I HAVEN'T HEARD. BUT WE SHOULD CELEBRATE ANYWAY!

WE TIED IT WITH TWINE AND HID IT IN HERE.
BUT IT ESCAPED TWO DAYS LATER AND NEVER REAPPEARED.

MOST CASES INVOLVE MEMORY LOSS SURROUNDING IMPORTANT DETAILS SUCH AS THE ALIEN'S APPEARANCE.
BUT I WISH WE AT LEAST KNEW WHETHER IT WAS A *GRAY* OR A *REPTILIAN*.
DO YOU REMEMBER WHAT IT LOOKED LIKE?
WELL, SORT OF, BUT...
YEAH, UM...

D...
DID IT...
Like this?
Or like this?
...LOOK LIKE EITHER OF THESE?

UMMM...
KAORINE WANTED TO GET INTO ART SCHOOL.
IT WAS LIKE THIS.

CHIRR CHIRR CHIRR CHIRR CHIRR CHIRR CHIRR CHIRR CHIRR

CHEER UP...
...OJIRO!
WE DIDN'T EXPECT THAT MUCH ANYWAY.
BUT I THINK THIS IS AN IMPORTANT DISCOVERY.

SURE...
THANKS, MAKOTO.
THE INVADERS WERE HERE EIGHT YEARS AGO!
ISN'T THAT WEIRD? IT MAKES ME WONDER!
ビールあります
大人
子供

YOU...
...MUST HAVE REALIZED IT WAS AN INVADER AFTER 8/31.
WHY DIDN'T YOU TELL ANYONE?
WE HAVE BEER
FROZEN
WELL...
...WE DID A LITTLE, BUT...

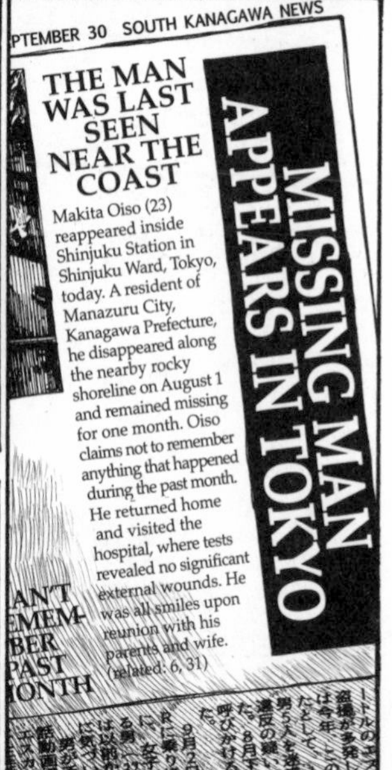

PTEMBER 30 SOUTH KANAGAWA NEWS

MISSING MAN APPEARS IN TOKYO

THE MAN WAS LAST SEEN NEAR THE COAST

Makita Oiso (23) reappeared inside Shinjuku Station in Shinjuku Ward, Tokyo, today. A resident of Manazuru City, Kanagawa Prefecture, he disappeared along the nearby rocky shoreline on August 1 and remained missing for one month. Oiso claims not to remember anything that happened during the past month. He returned home and visited the hospital, where tests revealed no significant external wounds. He was all smiles upon reunion with his parents and wife. (related: 6, 31)

AN'T REMEM-BER PAST ONTH

I REMEMBER BEING DRUNK AND FALLING ASLEEP ON THE BEACH...

...BUT WHEN I WOKE UP, I WAS AT SHINJUKU STATION.

I HAD LOST A WHOLE MONTH.

AND MY WALLET AND PHONE WERE GONE. IT WAS AWFUL.

MY HEAD FELT FUNNY, AND I DIDN'T LIKE IT AT ALL.

I SHOULD PROBABLY GET CHECKED OUT AT THE HOSPITAL AGAIN.

HYPER MYSTERY MY

MAKITA! READY TO GO?

I HAVEN'T TOLD MY WIFE ABOUT THIS...

...SO I SHOULD GET GOING.

OJIRO...

...I'M CERTAIN...
...THAT MAN ENCOUNTERED THE INVADER FROM THE TUNNEL.

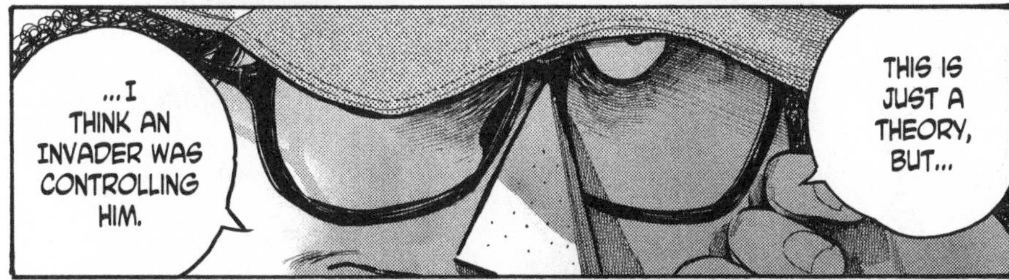
THIS IS JUST A THEORY, BUT...
...I THINK AN INVADER WAS CONTROLLING HIM.

BUT I'VE NEVER HEARD OF INVADERS DOING THAT.
WHAT IF THEY'RE POSSESSING PEOPLE...
...AND INFILTRATING HUMAN SOCIETY?!

HA HA... KENTARO...
THE INVADERS CAN'T-

UH...

OJIRO!! I'VE REWORKED THE ARTICLE...

...BUT I NEED TO DO MORE RESEARCH!!

I...
...DON'T KNOW MUCH, BUT...
...I THINK THEY WERE OUR *INVESTIGATORS*.

INVESTIGATORS?
INVESTIGATING *WHAT?*

THIS...
...WAS PLANNED A LONG TIME AGO.

PLANNED?

WHAT DO YOU INVADERS...
...REALLY WANT?!

DE DE DE DE DE DE DE DE DE DE DE DE DE DE DE DE DE DE DE DE DE DE DE DE DE DE DE DE DE DE DE DE DE DE DE DE DE DE DE DE DE DE

DE DE DE DE DE

CHAPTER 54

WHAT DO YOU INVADERS...
...REALLY WANT?!

UM...

OR WERE YOU DUMB ENOUGH TO COME HERE...
...TO ACTUALLY *INVADE*...
...DESPITE BEING WEAK AND UNARMED?

SKWAWK SKWAWK SKWAWK SKWAWK SKWAWK SKWAWK

THE INVESTI-GATORS...
...MAY HAVE MADE A MISTAKE.
THE ADULTS SAID THAT...
...HUMANITY HAD GROWN UP ACCORDING TO THE PLAN, SO WE SHOULD HAVE BEEN ABLE TO GET ALONG WITH THEM.

GROWN UP?

THEY ALL...
...CALLED THIS PLACE *HOME*.

AND HUMAN BEINGS...
...WERE LIKE *LIVESTOCK* TO PURIFY OUR HOME'S CONTAMINATED AIR.

ONTAN!
IT'S DARK, SO WE'RE GOING BACK!
FOOWAH!

I'M SORRY.

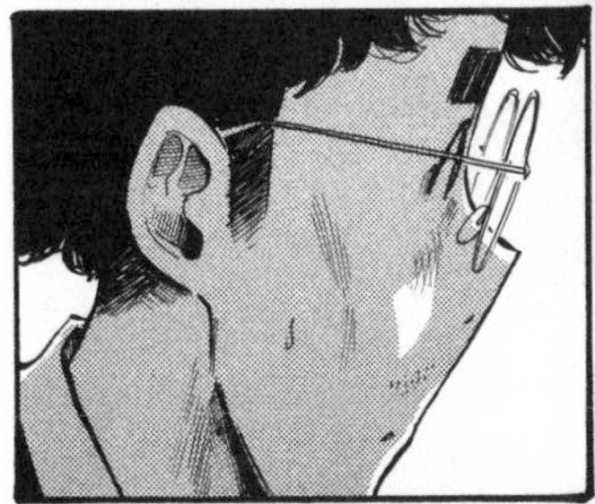

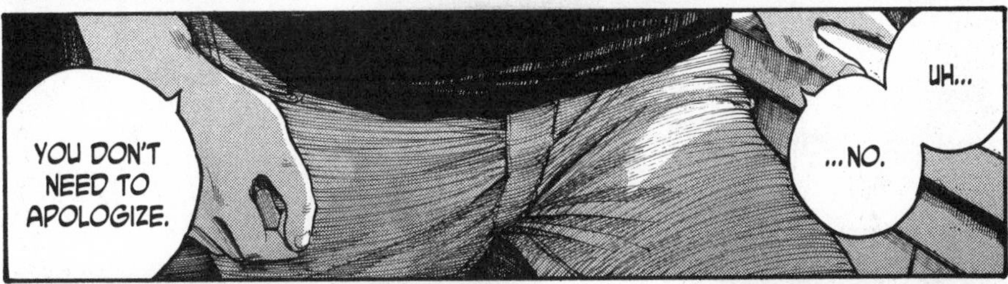
UH...
...NO.
YOU DON'T NEED TO APOLOGIZE.

SIGH...
WHAT-EVER.
ENOUGH OF THAT CONVER-SATION.
I DON'T GET IT...
...BUT I SORT OF DO!

IT'S ABOUT TIME FOR DINNER.
WHAT DO YOU WANT TO EAT?
HM? I WANT SASHIMI!
SOUNDS GOOD. GO CALL THE GIRLS.

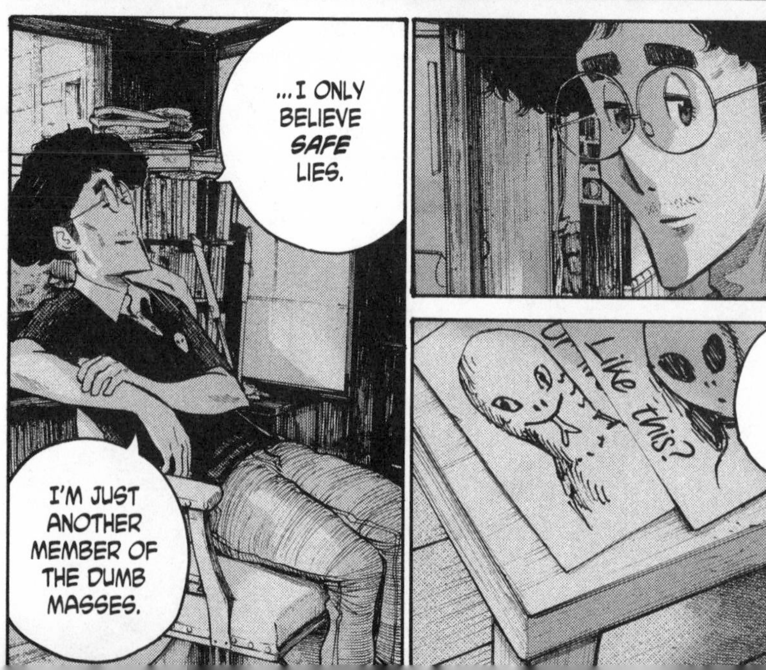

DEAD DEAD DEMON'S DEDEDEDE DESTRUCTION

CHIRR CHIRR CHIRR CHIRR CHIRR CHIRR CHIRR CHIRR CHIRR

I WISH SUMMER VACATION WOULD NEVER END.

HELP ME WITH LAUNDRY ...

...AND STOP TALKING LIKE *DEBEKO*.

CHIRR CHIRR CHIRR

AH HA HA!!
WA-HOO!!

I'M *BORED*.

YOU SHOULD GO SWIM, MAKOTO!

I TOLD YOU.

MY WIG WOULD COME OFF.

I DON'T THINK ANYONE WOULD MIND.
SERI-OUSLY?
YOU DON'T KNOW HOW HARD THIS IS FOR ME.

I ENVY YOU, OBA!
YOU'VE GOT AN IDOL'S GOOD LOOKS...
...AND YOU'RE SPACEY. NOT A CARE IN THE WORLD!

WAH!
EVEN I HAVE THINGS I CAN'T REVEAL.
HUH? DON'T BE SO VAGUE.
WE'RE BOTH GUYS, SO BE OPEN WITH ME.
HEY...
MAKOTO, CAN YOU KEEP A SECRET?
YEAH!!
OF COURSE!

TA-DA!
I'M ACTUALLY AN INVADER.

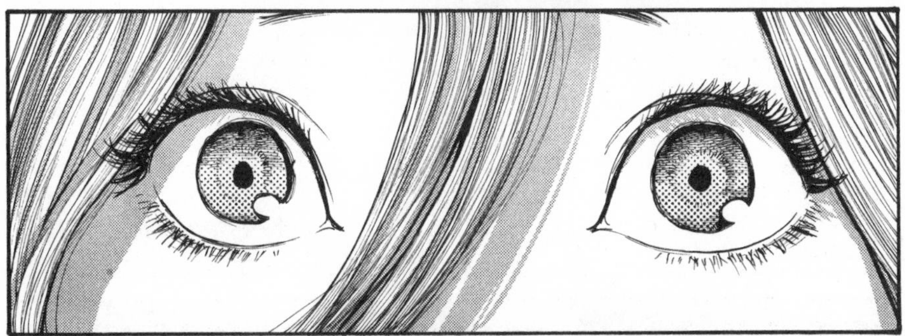

GAH!!
W-W-WHOA!!
OBA!!
DON'T SHOW THAT!!

OH, OKAY...

...G-GOT IT.

ARE YOU...

...SCARED OF ME NOW?

S...

SCARED?

OF COURSE I'M NOT SCARED!
FUTABA TAUGHT ME TO ABANDON PREJUDICE AND BE FAIR!!

GOOD.

I THINK I FINALLY UNDER-STAND...
...WHY ORAN LIKES YOU.

BUT THAT'S GONNA BE...
...YOU KNOW...
...NOT EASY.
UM...
...I CAN'T EXPLAIN IT WELL, BUT...

... ANYWAY ...
...BE KIND TO HER.
AFTER ALL, SHE IS A GIRL.

I'M COMIN' IN!!

OH! MAKOTO'S HERE!!

OBA.

ORAN?

YOU'RE DONE SWIMMING?

MAKOTO WANTED TO GO OUT TO THE OCEAN.

BUT DEEP WATER IS TOO MUCH FOR ME!!

I'M IN OVER MY HEAD AS IT IS, TAKING CARE OF MY FREE-LOADING BROTHER!!

WAH!

OH, I GET IT.

MAKOTO'S QUITE DEVIOUS!

HUH?

ORAN...

...LET'S TAKE A WALK.

CHIRR
CHIRR CHIRR
CHIRR CHIRR
CHIRR CHIRR
CHIRR CHIRR

OBA...
...I'M KINDA THIRSTY.

ORAN!
WAS THAT A HINT?

SHUT UP!
JUST BUY ME SOMETHING!

WHOA...

DEDEDEDE!!
DEAD DEAD
DEMON'S
DEDE
DEDE
DESTRUCTION

DE

MAYBE IT CRASHED IN TOKYO BAY AND DRIFTED HERE.

THE SDF'S SUCCESS RATE IS ALMOST 100 PERCENT.

PSHAW! DON'T BELIEVE THE GOVERNMENT, OBA.

SOMEBODY MAY STILL BE INSIDE.

CHAPTER 55

OBA...

...YOU'RE STARTING TO SOUND *HUMAN*.

ISOBEYAN
NOPE!!
NO ONE'S HOME!!

THEY MUST'VE RUN OFF.
SO THEY'RE ALL RIGHT.
PROB-ABLY.

ORAN...

RECENTLY ...
...I DON'T KNOW WHO I AM ANYMORE.
IT'S STRANGE.
WAS I REALLY AN INVADER?

BUT...
...I TOOK CONTROL OF THIS BODY...
...AND NOW MAYBE IT'S RECLAIMING ITSELF.
AM I STILL REALLY ME?
WELL, HUMANS CAN'T POP OPEN THEIR HEADS!
WAH!
RIGHT.

IS THE ORIGINAL OBA COMING BACK?
KADODE LIKES THAT AIRHEAD, BUT...

I DON'T KNOW.
I DON'T KNOW, BUT...

...HUMAN BEINGS ARE THE STRONGEST CREATURES IN EXISTENCE.
THEY'RE CUNNING AND HIGHLY PROCREATIVE.
BEFORE LONG, THEY'LL PROBABLY CONQUER THE UNIVERSE.

UGH.
I DID *NOT* NEED TO KNOW THAT.

IT'S A BUMMER...
...AND IT'S *DISGUSTING.*
YOU INVADERS ALWAYS STIR UP TROUBLE.

SORRY.

OBA, YOU SHOULDN'T APOLOGIZE SO MUCH.
LET'S GO BACK.
I HAVE TO LEARN HOW TO DO THE FORWARD CRAWL SO FAST IT *KILLS* PEOPLE!

HEY, ORAN?

IF YOU HAD A TIME MACHINE...
...AND YOU COULD RELIVE YOUR LIFE...
...WOULD YOU DO IT?

OBA, I'M NOT A CHILD...
...SO I DON'T ENTERTAIN SUCH FANTASIES.

BUT SUPPOSE THERE WOULDN'T BE ANY INVADERS.
WOULD YOU DO IT?

IN THAT CASE...
...*YOU* WOULDN'T BE THERE EITHER.

WAH!
THAT'S RIGHT.
BECAUSE I'M AN INVADER.

Please do not leave pet waste, fish hooks, fishing line or other trash on the beach.

OBA...

YES?

I LOOO-OOVE ...

...YOU-UUUU!!

ME, TOO.

I LOVE...
...YOU.

SO...
...DON'T DISAPPEAR ALL OF A SUDDEN, OKAY?
DON'T...
...GO ANYWHERE.

I...

HEEEY!!
WE'RE GOING BACK!
ARGH! A BOY AND GIRL ALONE TOGETHER!!
I BET THEY WERE DOING SOMETHING *SHAMEFUL*!!
KADODE, YOU...

HYA HYA FOOWAH!

I hate summer.

8/32
was like an
unending
summer...

...and the
end of the
world.

THE TOPIC.

S.E.S.

TELL ME THE TRUTH.

WHAT IS S.E.S.'S TRUE OBJECTIVE?

IT'S WEIRD FOR S.E.S.'S ROBOTICS DIVISION TO BRING IN AN OUTSIDER LIKE TAKARADA AS PRODUCT MANAGER.

AND HE KNOWS TOO MUCH ABOUT THE INVADERS AND THE MOTHER SHIP.

COULD IT BE...

...THAT HE'S AN INVADER?

GASP!
THAT'S RIDICULOUS!
HE JOINED THE COMPANY SIX YEARS AGO!
THAT WAS *BEFORE* 8/31!

I THOUGHT YOU CAME TO TALK ABOUT FUJIN BEING USED IN NURSING-WELFARE FIELDS.
SHOULD I CALL SECURITY?

MAYBE THE INVADERS WERE HERE PRIOR TO 8/31.
MR. TAKARADA IS A HARD-WORKING RESEARCHER.
IF YOU'RE SO MISTRUSTFUL OF TALENT...
...THEN YOU'RE A *SMALL* MAN.

BIASED RESEARCHERS SHOULDN'T GO SNOOPING AROUND.
THE MEDIA IS ALWAYS LOOKING FOR SOMEONE TO BLAME...
...BUT IF YOU INTERFERE WITH MY WORK, YOU'RE MY ENEMY.

MR. MIURA...
...DON'T BOTHER ME EVER AGAIN.
WE ARE HONESTLY STRIVING TO BUILD HUMANITY'S FUTURE.

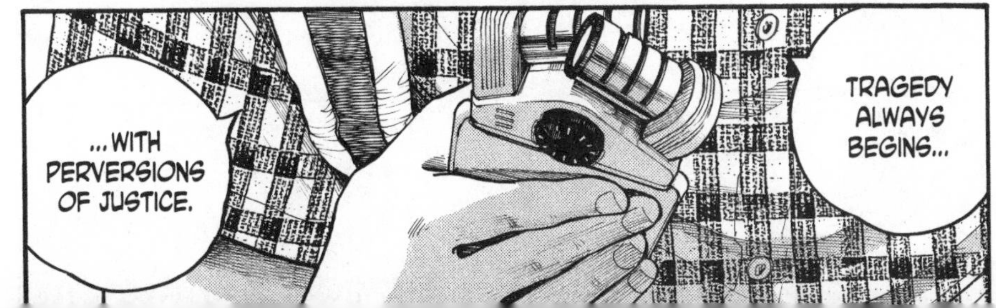
TRAGEDY ALWAYS BEGINS...
...WITH PERVERSIONS OF JUSTICE.

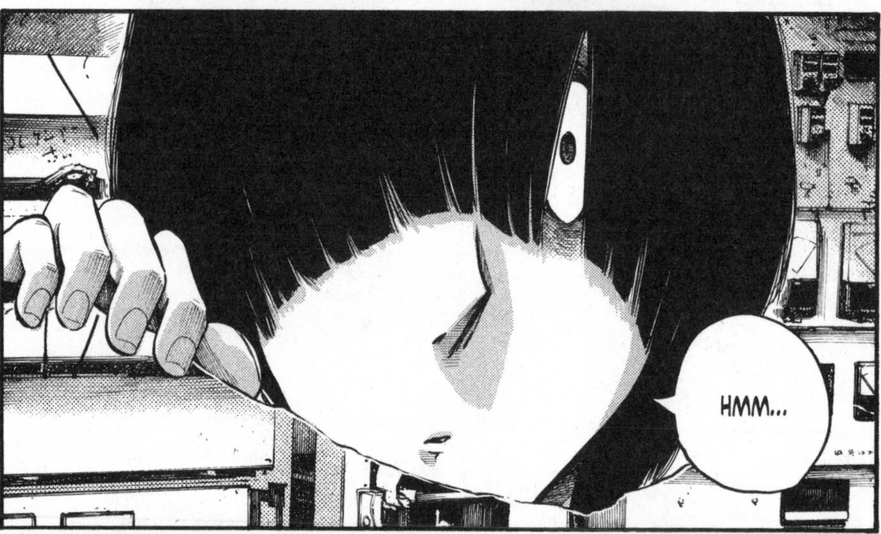
HMM...

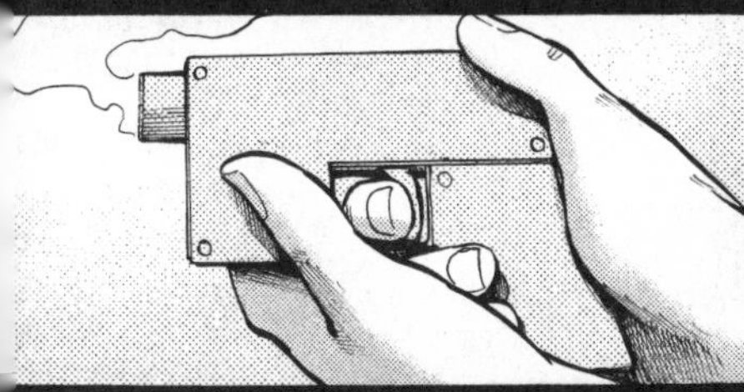

DEAD DEAD DEMON'S DEDEDEDE DESTRUCTION

YATTSUKE RECORDS
RESIST SHIP
RESIST SHIP
RESIST
D...
DIRECTOR?!
YOU SAID WE DIDN'T HAVE TO KILL HIM!!
TAKARADA IS LEADING THE WORLD ASTRAY.
SO WE MUST STOP HIM.
EVEN IF IT MEANS...
... COMMITTING HEINOUS ACTS.
GSDF × S.E.S

ARE YOU NOT...
...BRAVE ENOUGH FOR THAT?
IT'S JUST...
...PLAYING AT REVOLUTION...
...ANYWAY.
YOU'RE ALREADY ONE OF US...
...AND WE WILL NOT ABIDE BETRAYAL.
GAH !!

CHIRR
CHIRR
CHIRR

BYE, GIRLS!
WE'LL NEVER FORGET YOU!!
I'LL DEFINITELY WRITE YOU!!
GROUP TEXTS ARE GOOD ENOUGH!
BYE-BYE!

I'LL DRIVE THEM TO THE STATION.
THE REST OF YOU KEEP UP THE RESEARCH!
YOU'RE LEAVING TOO, FUTABA?
UH... YEAH.
I LEAVE THIS EVENING.

THIS IS JUST A THEORY, BUT...
...THE INVADERS MAY BE MESSENGERS FROM BEINGS ON A HIGHER PLANE.
THEY MAY BE A KIND OF CATALYST, PARASITIZING US AND RAISING US TO A HIGHER DIMENSION.

HUMANITY'S *ASCENSION* HAS BEGUN!

WAH!

I CAN'T SAY FOR SURE, BUT I DOUBT THAT.

DO YOU HAVE A MINUTE?

CHIRR CHIRR
CHIRR CHIRR CHIRR
CHIRR CHIRR CHIRR
CHIRR CHIRR CHIRR
CHIRR CHIRR CHIRR

HMM...

SORRY, BUT...
...YOU'RE THE ONLY ONE I COULD TELL.
BUT MAYBE YOU ALREADY GUESSED.

DO YOU HAVE BULLETS?
THERE ARE THREE IN HERE.
BUT THE GUN CAN ONLY FIRE ONCE. THE PLASTIC ISN'T DURABLE.
KAMEIDO'S IN A RUSH!

STUDENTS ENGAGING IN SOCIAL ACTIVISM IS ONE THING...
...BUT THIS IS JUST *TERRORISM*.
I DON'T THINK...
...THEY'LL ACTUALLY SHOOT ANYONE.
THEY JUST WANT TO CREATE A SCARE AT THE UNVEILING OF THE NEW STADIUM.

SO YOU WANT ME...
...TO KEEP IT UNTIL EVERYTHING BLOWS OVER?

YEAH, SORRY.
JUST HAVING IT IS SCARY.

CAN'T YOU JUST APOLOGIZE AND GIVE IT BACK?
IF I CROSS THEM NOW, THEY'LL RETALIATE.

IF SOMETHING HAPPENS, THERE WILL BE ARRESTS...
...AND S.H.I.P. WILL BREAK UP.
I MIGHT BE ABLE TO ESCAPE IN THE CONFUSION...
...AND THEN I CAN GET RID OF THE GUN.

FINE.
BUT PROMISE ME SOME-THING.

YES?

LEARN A LESSON FROM THIS.

I WILL!!

TAKE CARE, FUTABA!
THANKS FOR COMING!
FUTABA!
I'LL LET YOU KNOW WHEN I GET BACK!

YEAH... SEE YOU IN TOKYO.

SKWAWK SKWAWK
SKWAWK SKWAWK
SKWAWK SKWAWK
SKWAWK SKWAWK

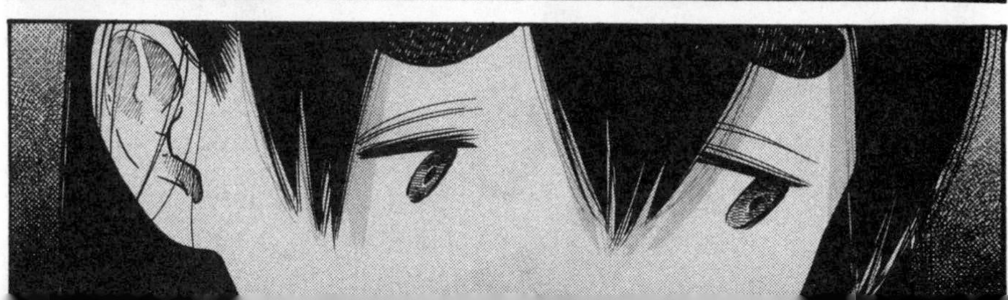

CLATTER

MAKOTO!
WAKE UP!
WHAT DO YOU WANT?
ORAN WENT OUTSIDE ALONE!
SO? WHAT TIME IS IT?

FORGET YOUR BAG AND LET'S GO!
SHE PROBABLY JUST WENT TO LAY A BOOBY TRAP AS A GAG OR SOMETHING...

HAVE YOU CALLED HER?

SHE ISN'T ANSWERING!!

HUH?

I SAW IT...

...WHEN I USED THIS MEMORY-READING MACHINE.

SHE'S A *TIME TRAVELER*.

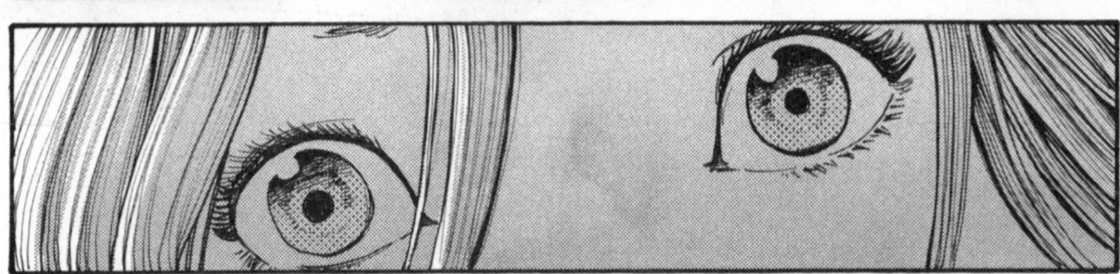

THIS IS AN INVADER DEVICE.
IT READS PEOPLE'S MEMORIES.
I USED IT ON ORAN...
...SO HER CHILDHOOD MEMORIES ARE STILL IN HERE.

IF WE PLAY THEM BACK, WE CAN RELIVE THEM.
THEN WE'LL SEE...
...WHAT HAPPENED TO ORAN AND KADODE EIGHT YEARS AGO.

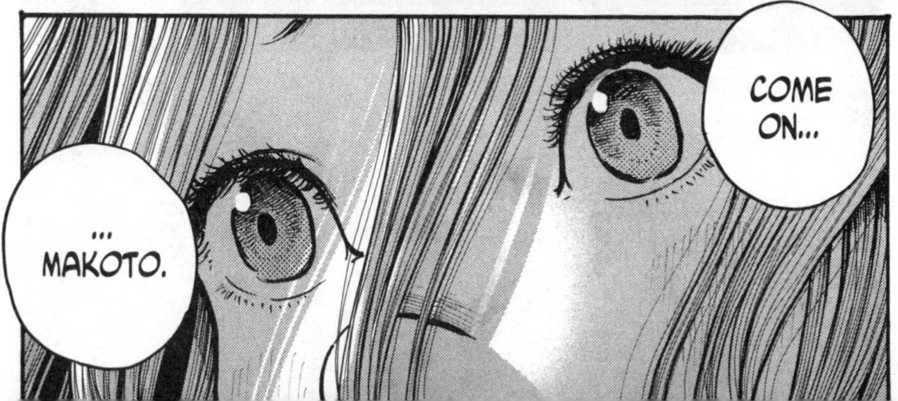
COME ON...
...MAKOTO.

I'LL TEACH YOU...

...THE TRUTH.

THIS IS CNC HOT TOPIX NEWS!
GOOD EVENING, I'M ROBERT FRANKLIN!
NOW, IN NEWS FROM THE WHITE HOUSE!

PRESIDENT PADRON HELD A PRESS CONFERENCE...
...AND CLAIMED TO HAVE PROOF THAT THE MOTHER SHIP IS GOING TO EXPLODE.
Today's President
LIVE

IF SNEAKY JAPAN DOESN'T GIVE UP ITS MONOPOLY OVER THE MOTHER SHIP, WE'RE GOING TO HAVE TO...
...AMERICA IS GOING TO LAUNCH A PREEMPTIVE STRIKE ON THAT THING LIKE YOU WOULDN'T BELIEVE, LIKE YOU'VE NEVER SEEN BEFORE!

HEY, SEAN?
IS THIS REALLY HAPPENING?

STOP
YEAH.
EARTH IS SO *SCREWED*.

DEDEDEDE

Dead Dead Demon's
Dedededede Destruction Volume 7
Inio Asano

Background Assistants: Ran Atsumori
Miki Imai
CG: Naoto Tomita

THIS RING IS GREAT, YO!
SORRY, BUT CHECK THIS OUT, YO!
UM, UM...
...HOLD ON A SEC!
BLAH BLAH BLAH BLAH ...
What?

PEOPLE ARE TOO SMALL-MINDED TO UNDERSTAND ME.
I BET ANIMALS WOULD LOVE ME!
DEBEKO, YOU NEED HELP.
HIYA, CUTE PUPPY!
CONSOLE ME WITH YOUR PURE HEART!
YOUR FACE LOOKS LIKE **ASS.**
YOU NEED TO REROLL!

DEAD DEAD DEMON'S DEDEDEDE DESTRUCTION

Volume 7

VIZ Signature Edition

Story and Art by **Inio Asano**

Translation **John Werry**

Touch-Up Art & Lettering **Annaliese Christman**

Design **Shawn Carrico**

Editor **Pancha Diaz**

Original Cover Design:
Kaoru KUROKI·Chie SATO+Bay Bridge Studio

Printed in Canada

Published by VIZ Media, LLC
P.O. Box 77010
San Francisco, CA 94107

10 9 8 7 6 5 4 3 2 1
First printing, October 2019

viz.com

VIZ SIGNATURE
vizsignature.com

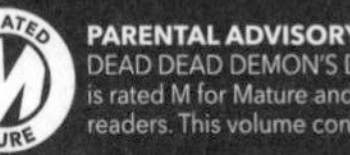